j 968
J D29x

CL

AGIF7947-1

LOBEDU

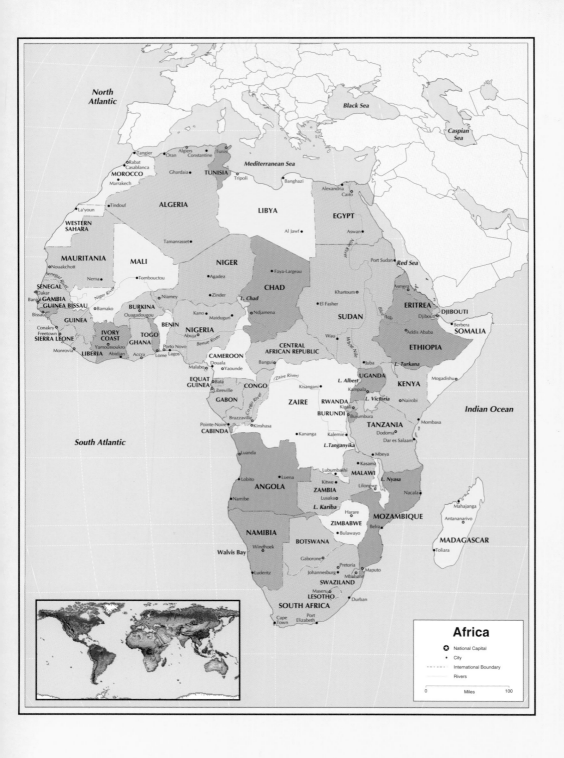

North
Atlantic

Black Sea

Caspian
Sea

MOROCCO
Tangier
Rabat
Casablanca
Marrakech
Algiers
Oran Constantine
Ghardaia
Tunis
TUNISIA
Tripoli
Mediterranean Sea
Banghazi
Alexandria
Cairo

WESTERN
SAHARA
La'youn
Tindouf

ALGERIA

LIBYA

EGYPT

Aswan

Tamanrasset
Al Jawf

MAURITANIA
Nouakchott
Nema

MALI
Tombouctou
NIGER
Agadez
Zinder
Niamey
L. Chad
CHAD
Faya-Largeau

Port Sudan
Red Sea

SENEGAL
Dakar
Banjul
GAMBIA
GUINEA BISSAU
Bissau

Senegal River
Niger River
Bamako
BURKINA
Ouagadougou

Kano
Maiduguri
Ndjamena

Khartoum
El Fasher
SUDAN

Asmera
ERITREA
Djibouti
DJIBOUTI
Addis Ababa
SOMALIA
Berbera

GUINEA
Conakry
Freetown
SIERRA LEONE
Monrovia
LIBERIA

IVORY
COAST
Yamoussoukro
GHANA
Abidjan
Accra
BENIN
TOGO
Porto Novo
Lome Lagos
NIGERIA
Abuja
Benue River

CAMEROON
Malabo
Douala
Yaounde

CENTRAL
AFRICAN REPUBLIC
Bangui

Wau
White Nile
Black Nile
Nile River

ETHIOPIA
L. Turkana

Juba
UGANDA
L. Albert
Kampala
KENYA
Mogadishu

EQUAT.
GUINEA
Bata
Libreville
CONGO
GABON

Kisangani

(Zaire River)

Orange Nile River

ZAIRE
Brazzaville
Pointe-Noire
Kinshasa
CABINDA

RWANDA
Kigali
BURUNDI
Bujumbura
L. Victoria
Nairobi

TANZANIA
Dodoma
Dar es Salaam
Mombasa

Indian Ocean

South Atlantic

Kanonga
Kalemie
L.Tanganyika

Mbeya
Kasama

Luanda
Lobito
Luena
Lubumbashi
Kitwe
MALAWI
Lilongwe
L. Nyasa
Nacala

ANGOLA
Namibe

ZAMBIA
Lusaka
L. Kariba

MOZAMBIQUE
Mahajanga
Antananarivo

NAMIBIA
Windhoek
Walvis Bay
Luderitz

BOTSWANA
Gaborone

Harare
ZIMBABWE
Bulawayo
Beira

MADAGASCAR
Toliara

Johannesburg
Pretoria
Maputo
Mbabane
SWAZILAND
Maseru
LESOTHO
Durban
SOUTH AFRICA
Cape
Town
Port
Elizabeth

Africa

✪ National Capital
• City
- - - - International Boundary
—— Rivers

0   Miles   100

LOBEDU

Patricia Davison, Ph.D.

THE ROSEN PUBLISHING GROUP, INC.
NEW YORK

Published in 1998 by The Rosen Publishing Group, Inc.
29 East 21st Street, New York, NY 10010

Copyright 1998 by The Rosen Publishing Group, Inc.

First Edition

Manufactured in the United States of America

Library of Congress Cataloging-in-Publication Data

Davison, Patricia.
    Lobedu/Patricia Davison.
       p.   cm. — (The heritage library of African peoples)
    Includes bibliographical references and index.
    Summary: Surveys the history, culture, and contemporary life of the Lobedu people of South Africa.
    ISBN 0-8239-1989-7
    1. Lobedu (African people)—Juvenile literature.   [1. Lobedu (African people)]   I. Title. II. Series.
DT920.D38   1998
968′.004963975—dc21   96-45308
                                               CIP
                                              AC

Contents

INTRODUCTION

THERE IS EVERY REASON FOR US TO KNOW something about Africa and to understand its past and the way of life of its peoples. Africa is a rich continent that has for centuries provided the world with art, culture, labor, wealth, and natural resources. It has vast mineral deposits, fossil fuels, and commercial crops.

But perhaps most important is the fact that fossil evidence indicates that human beings originated in Africa. The earliest traces of human beings and their tools are almost two million years old. Their descendants have migrated throughout the world. To be human is to be of African descent.

The experiences of the peoples who stayed in Africa are as rich and as diverse as of those who established themselves elsewhere. This series of books describes their environment, their modes of subsistence, their relationships, and their customs and beliefs. The books present the variety of languages, histories, cultures, and religions that are to be found on the African continent. They demonstrate the historical linkages between African peoples and the way contemporary Africa has been affected by European colonial rule.

Africa is large, complex, and diverse. It encompasses an area of more than 11,700,000 square miles. The United States, Europe, and India could fit easily into it. The sheer size is an indication of the continent's great variety in geography, terrain, climate, flora, fauna, peoples, languages, and cultures.

Much of contemporary Africa has been shaped by European colonial rule, industrialization, urbanization, and the demands of a world economic system. For more than seventy years, large regions of Africa were ruled by Great Britain, France, Belgium, Portugal, and Spain. African peoples from various ethnic, linguistic, and cultural backgrounds were brought together to form colonial states.

For decades Africans struggled to gain their independence. It was not until after World War II that the colonial territories became independent African states. Today, almost all of Africa is ruled by Africans. Large numbers of Africans live in modern cities. Rural Africa is also being transformed, and yet its people still engage in many of their customs and beliefs.

Contemporary circumstances and natural events have not always been kind to ordinary Africans. Today, however, new popular social movements and technological innovations pose great promise for future development.

George C. Bond, Ph.D., Director
Institute of African Studies
Columbia University, New York

The Lobedu are ruled by a queen who is believed to control the rain. At her royal capital, many important community events are held. This dancer is celebrating his graduation from a special Lobedu school for men.

chapter

1

PEOPLE OF THE RAIN QUEEN

THE PEOPLE KNOWN AS THE LOBEDU (pronounced loh-VHEH-doo) are widely known through the fame of their ruler, Modjadji (moh-JUDGE-ee), the Rain Queen. She lives in the Lobedu capital, called her *mosata*, or chief's place. It is located in the wooded foothills of the Drakensberg Mountains in the Northern Province of South Africa. This is the traditional center of Lobedu cultural life. Today many Lobedu people live in the capital and surrounding rural districts. Even those Lobedu who live in cities and other parts of the country generally still have links with Lobedu traditions. These traditions are centered on the Rain Queen.

Oral traditions record Lobedu history back to the 1500s. In that era the Karanga state, north of the Limpopo River in present-day Zimbabwe, was splitting apart. One group that broke away from a branch of the Karanga ruling family

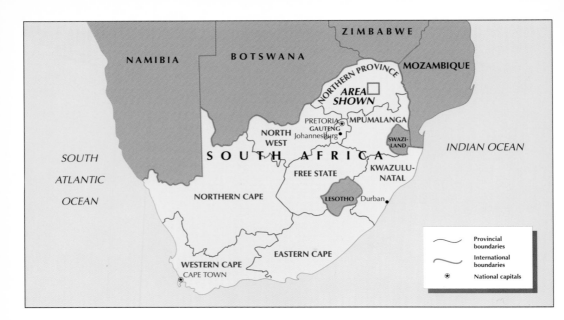

In the 1500s the Lobedu people migrated south of the Limpopo River, which forms the border between Zimbabwe and the Northern Province of South Africa. They settled in a small area of the Northern Province, known today as BoLobedu District. The Lobedu *mosata*, or royal capital, is usually referred to simply as Modjadji, after the ruler. The Lobedu also live and work in many other parts of South Africa.

migrated southward. They took with them the sacred beads of their ancestors and the secret knowledge of how to make rain.

These Karanga moved south of the Limpopo River and settled in an area that was rich in fruit-bearing trees and had fertile soil for planting grain crops. They absorbed the peoples already living in the region. According to legend, some of these earlier people were unable to make fire or forge iron tools. Others were farmers who lived in scattered groups. They were distantly related to the North Sotho people who are still found in this area today. Once they had settled, the Karanga immigrants gradually formed a new culture. They became Lobedu.

At about the same time, the Venda people, who had also moved southward from Zimbabwe, were establishing their own chiefdoms north of the Lobedu area. During the centuries that followed there were frequent social and trade contacts between the Lobedu and Venda.

The emerging Lobedu culture kept some parts of the Karanga culture. It also adopted practices from the neighboring Venda and Sotho peoples. The Lobedu share many cultural features with other peoples in southern Africa. But in Lobedu society the role of women, both as sisters and wives, developed a special character. Lobedu women had a high social status and played important roles both at home and in public.

The early Lobedu chiefs were all male. This practice lasted until the end of the 1700s. Then, a long period of internal dispute over royal succession occurred, followed by severe drought

Since the early 1800s the Lobedu have been ruled by a succession of female chiefs who have all been named Modjadji. Because these rulers are believed to have the spiritual power to cause rain to fall, they are called rain queens. Seen above is Rain Queen Modjadji IV. She is seated in a traditional pose on a mat on the veranda of her palace.

and famine. At this time a woman became chief. Her name was Modjadji. She was the daughter of Mogudo, a chief whose sons had been sent into exile. According to legend, Mogudo fathered a child with Modjadji to strengthen the royal line. This child, a daughter, eventually succeeded her mother as chief.

Modjadji restored peace and prosperity to her people. Her success brought her honor and power. People recognized her as the ruler of the Lobedu. The rain queen was believed to rule by divine right, meaning that her position was backed by ancestral spirits. She possessed spiritual power to make or withhold rain. These abilities were the vital source of her authority. Powerful chiefs from distant Zululand and Sekhukuniland paid homage to Modjadji, the Rain Queen, sending her tribute in return for rain. Since that time, despite major changes in the politics of South Africa, the Lobedu people have been ruled by a series of rain queens, all named Modjadji.

The present queen, Modjadji V, came to power in 1982. She rules in an era that is very different from those of earlier queens. Modern items such as television sets, cars, and the latest Western fashions are now common in traditional villages. Despite these outward changes, many Lobedu traditions have adapted to modern times and are still treasured. Since the 1960s, the pace

of technological change has been rapid. But the Lobedu have drawn on their traditions to keep their identity as the people of the rain queen. Since the coming of majority rule to South Africa in 1994, confidence in African cultural heritage increased and continues to grow. But there is also uncertainty about the future of traditional chiefs.

Today about 200,000 people live in Modjadji's territory. Less than 10 percent of them are descended from the original founding group. Nonetheless, the position of chief has remained in the royal line of the founding ancestors. Many people unrelated to the Lobedu settled in the area and regard Modjadji as their chief. However, some people of Lobedu origin live in other parts of South Africa and no longer observe the traditions of their ancestors.

▼ LANGUAGE ▼

The Lobedu language is one of a large group of African languages known as Bantu languages. The original language spoken by the Lobedu had no written form. It shared strong similarities with TshiVenda, the language of the nearby Venda people. It also contained elements of the languages spoken by neighboring North Sotho people.

When the Lobedu language was first put into writing, Lobedu words were spelled in several different ways. For example, Lobedu was usually written as Lovedu or Lovhedu, because the "b" sound was pronounced softly as "vh" in the original Lobedu dialect. Schools eventually adopted the standard North Sotho spelling of the dialect, and the written Lobedu language became known as SeLobedu. Though elderly people in rural villages still remember the old dialect, young Lobedu prefer to use the standardized language taught in schools.

As in all Bantu languages, a system of prefixes is used to change the meaning of a noun. For example, BaLobedu means the Lobedu people; BoLobedu refers to the geographical region where they live; and SeLobedu is their language.▲

chapter

2

HISTORY

DURING THE EARLY 1800S, MODJADJI I controlled the large area between the Great Letaba and Little Letaba Rivers and an extensive area beyond this. Beginning around 1840, waves of Tsonga-speaking people migrated into the area from the southeast and settled on the low-lying plains.

During the second half of the 1800s, white settlers moved into the Zoutpansberg district, which included Lobedu territory. They hunted for game in the area and sought to control Modjadji II, who ruled from 1854 to 1895. These settlers were mainly farmers of Dutch origin, or Boers. They had left the Cape Colony to avoid British rule.

Traveling by ox-wagon and on horseback, these Voortrekkers, as they became known, crossed the Vaal River and founded an independent republic in 1852. With the help of firearms, which made up for their small numbers, the Boers claimed land, labor, and taxes from the Lobedu and others living in the region. This began a long period of conflict.

As local chiefs resisted the threat to their land, the Boers used greater force. The Lobedu defended their territory with guns they obtained through trade. They also refused to pay taxes to the government of the Boer republic, called the South African Republic. In 1890 a commando force was sent to subdue the Lobedu and force them to pay taxes. The Lobedu people continued to fight back by setting fire to the Boers' houses and stealing their cattle.

Despite this vigorous defense, Modjadji's territory was eventually reduced to an area less than one-tenth of its original size. In 1892 this area was officially named the Modjadji Location.

The resistance of Modjadji II and neighboring chiefs was eventually crushed in 1894. A South African Republic military force on horseback attacked and burned the villages of rebellious chiefs. They entered Modjadji's capital and forced her people to surrender their guns and a large number of cattle.

Although the capital was not destroyed, the Lobedu were forced to pay a heavy fine in cattle and admit defeat. Still, Lobedu anger over the

In earlier times the court was held in the *khôrô* (above).

seizure of their land did not subside. Modjadji avoided the dishonor of appearing before the generals of the South African Republic by sending a stand-in dressed to look like her.

Amid the conflicts of the late 1800s, German missionaries established a settlement in Modjadji's area. These Christian missionaries experienced little early success. As time passed, however, the Lobedu began to tolerate Christian beliefs and eventually combined aspects of Christianity with their existing religious practices. A German missionary named Fritz Reuter tried without success to help the Lobedu people regain their land.

Modjadji II ended her reign in 1895 in the same manner as the previous queen—she committed suicide by taking poison in a solemn ceremony. Later rain queens did not follow this tradition.

By the early 1900s, the Lobedu people began to be drawn into the industrial economy of South Africa. A railway line connected the Lobedu area to the gold mining region around Johannesburg. Many Lobedu men became migrant workers in the mines in order to earn money to pay taxes and buy Western goods.

Land remained an important issue for the Lobedu. In 1913 the South African parliament passed the Native Land Act, which regulated where blacks were allowed to own land. The Modjadji Location became known as a "native reserve." In 1936 another law enlarged the reserve to twice its size. However, it allowed South Africa to remove blacks from areas reserved for whites. After 1948, when the conservative National Party came to power, segregation of black and white South Africans was more strictly enforced under the system of apartheid, which means separateness.

The introduction of new apartheid laws in the 1950s put increasing pressure on the lives of the Lobedu people. More and more blacks were forced to move from areas that these laws reserved for whites.

The royal reception house of the rain queens was built in 1927. It is used for formal meetings with visitors.

In 1951 the Bantu Authorities Act set up a system of tribal, regional, and territorial authorities. Under this system white authorities administered and controlled the black population. This structure formed the foundation of the "homeland" policy. On the basis of ethnic differences, black South Africans were divided into eight "nations," each with its own homeland.

Black people were forced to become citizens of these artificial homelands, and they were denied South African citizenship. The homeland policy was also used to control the growing number of blacks who were living and working in towns. They could be forced to return to their rural homelands. This system meant that urban blacks were only temporary residents in the white-controlled cities that depended on their labor. If their labor was not required, they could be forced to move to a homeland.

In the Lobedu area white officials were appointed as administrators in 1958. This undermined the authority of traditional Lobedu chiefs, councillors, and headmen. A modern courthouse was built outside Modjadji's capital to replace the traditional court.

In the 1970s the Lobedu reserve was forced to become part of the North Sotho homeland, Lebowa, which was governed by a legislative assembly in Pietersburg. Modjadji was represented in this assembly by her brother. It also included representatives of a number of other Sotho-speaking groups, such as the Pedi. Although Lebowa was supposed to be self-governing, it remained economically dependent on South Africa. It also lacked the support of the people living there.

The apartheid system remained in place until 1994, when South Africa held its first democratic election that allowed blacks to vote. In post-apartheid South Africa, the former homelands have been abolished. Now all South Africans have full citizenship and equal rights. Since 1994 the Lobedu area has been part of the Northern Province of unified South Africa.▲

chapter

3

ENVIRONMENT

THE LANDSCAPE OF BOLOBEDU, THE REGION where the Lobedu live, varies from forested hills to river valleys and flat plains. The vegetation is bushveld savanna, a type of environment rich in trees, shrubs, creepers, and grasses.

The fertile, reddish soil is suitable for growing grain. However, at least two-thirds of the area is too steep for using an ox-drawn plow.

The climate is subtropical, and temperatures are seldom very high or very low. It rains in the hot summer months, and the winters are cool and dry. Disease-bearing insects, such as the malaria mosquito and tsetse fly, are common in the area, especially during the summer. In fact, the high risk of malaria discouraged whites from settling and trading in the regions surrounding the Lobedu district. The widespread use of pesticides in the 1950s, however, reduced disease and opened the region for farming.

The type of vegetation in the Lobedu area, known as bushveld savanna, includes trees, shrubs, grasses, and creepers. Seen above is a hill covered with trees called cycads.

In the past elephants, lions, several kinds of antelope, and other game animals thrived in the Lobedu area. Ivory was both an important symbol of prestige and an item of trade. Hunting game with traditional weapons did not seriously deplete the animal population. Later, however, the use of firearms drastically reduced the number of animals. Eventually laws were passed to restrict further hunting. Game reserves were formed to protect the remaining animals.

A magnificent forest of tall cycads, a rare type of tree that dates back millions of years, grows on a hillside close to the Lobedu capital. This

23

The cycad forest, seen above, is associated with the rain queen.

ancient forest has always been protected by the rain queens. The Lobedu people associate the cycad forest with Modjadji and therefore treat it with great respect. In 1936 it was declared a national monument, and in 1979 it became known as the Modjadji Nature Reserve. Today the cycad forest attracts tourism, which helps the local economy. In the valley below the capital, a project was set up to grow and sell cycads.

▼ SETTLEMENT ▼
Traditionally the Lobedu lived in family homesteads spread out over the hillsides, which

Seen here is the homestead of the Mathega family. It consists of several separate structures. The tree in the courtyard grows from the center of the family shrine.

were terraced with stone walls and used for farming. Because of land shortages, settlements have now spread to the valleys and plains. Homesteads have become smaller as large extended families have become less common. Most homesteads now have between two and ten houses.

According to customs still sometimes followed today, when a woman marries she moves from her family home to that of her husband. A wealthy man might have more than one wife, a practice known as polygyny. Although there is no limit to the number of wives a husband can

25

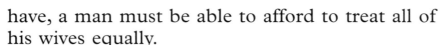

have, a man must be able to afford to treat all of his wives equally.

In the past a husband also had to pay a bride-price of cattle to each bride's family. This payment did not imply that the wife was bought. Instead, it compensated her family for losing a productive member of their group. It also acknowledged their input in raising her and the fact that she would provide children to her husband's family.

Today a polygynous household consists of a man, his wives, and their children. The man's mother might also live with them. Within the homestead each married woman has her own cooking house, sleeping house, and domestic courtyard. There is no strict ranking in the arrangement of houses within the settlement. A family shrine is usually placed in the courtyard of the senior wife.

Unlike the layout of other homesteads, Modjadji's capital (*mosata*) is a densely packed settlement. It is both a political center and the home of the royal family. It consists of more than 200 dwellings clustered around a central courtyard, the *khôrô*.

▼ *KHÔRÔ* POLE FIGURES ▼

The *khôrô* is surrounded by a palisade, or high fence, of carved poles, which are found only at the courts of headmen and district chiefs. These

This photograph of the palisade at the capital, taken in the 1960s, shows a number of carved poles.

poles therefore mark a place of authority among the Lobedu and related people of the Northern Province of South Africa.

Modjadji's *khôrô* is a circular arena that was traditionally used for hearing court cases, for public gatherings, and for ceremonial performances. Although the court was the domain of men, Modjadji was acknowledged as the head of the *khôrô*.

In the past, whenever the palisade was restored, men from all the districts that owed allegiance to Modjadji were expected to bring poles to the capital. Only men worked as carvers in the Lobedu culture. Through their skillfully

27

BELIEFS AND VALUES

Lobedu who follow tradition strictly—which few do today—believe in a creator called Khuzwane. Khuzwane is regarded as being far removed from everyday life. The ancestors, on the other hand, are intimately involved with the fortunes of their living relatives. They are responsible for health, good crops, and prosperity. If neglected, they show their displeasure by causing sickness, drought, or misfortune. Certain objects, such as old beads or iron tools, are believed to have links with the ancestors and must be carefully looked after.

The usual way of approaching or thanking the ancestors is by placing a small offering of beer or grain on a shrine. A shrine is often a small circular mound of clay, which is built in the courtyard of the homestead. Sometimes there are separate shrines for maternal and paternal ancestors. An object of religious importance, such as an iron hoe that has been handed down from one generation to the next, is buried inside the shrine. Families pay respect to their ancestors at these shrines. Modjadji alone has access to and is able to communicate with the royal ancestors on behalf of the entire nation.

According to past Lobedu customs, certain medicines had the power to control negative forces. Villages were usually protected by medicines that were buried around the perimeter and at the entrance. People who were considered to be spiritually impure could be treated with medicines to cleanse and make them healthy. Spiritual powers could be used for evil purposes, but charms or medicines could counteract ill will. It was also believed that evil could be caused by jealousy, so great emphasis was placed on cooperation and social harmony. Some of these beliefs continue today.

Diviners, often from outside the local community, were—and sometimes still are—called in to diagnose the cause of an illness or misfortune and prescribe a cure. To do this the diviner threw a set of bones, which included animal bones, shells, and other objects, onto a grass mat and then diagnosed the cause of the problem based on the position of the pieces. The cure usually involved the use of medicines and protective charms.

carved poles, carvers would both show their abilities and honor the chief. Collectively the poles of the *khôrô* expressed the solidarity of the different groups within Modjadji's territory. They were visual reminders of social and political ties among the Lobedu people.

Pole figures follow the long, thin shape of the pole itself. The actual carving is always located at the top of the pole. Although most poles had pointed or forked ends, some were carved in the form of human figures, animals, weapons, or utensils. These were found near the *khôrô* entrance and the opening in the palisade that led to Modjadji's private area. Although they were carved by men, many of the poles depicted women and activities associated with them. This suggests that the poles are symbols of the important roles played by women in Lobedu society.

Today court cases are heard in a modern building instead of in the *khôrô*. Men of the districts in Modjadji's territory still bring pointed poles to the royal *khôrô*, but pole figures are rarely seen.▲

chapter

4

WORK

ORAL ACCOUNTS ABOUT THE PAST SUGGEST that the Lobedu economy depended on the farming of sorghum and millet, two kinds of grain. The people also gathered wild fruits and insects for food. Beginning in the 1500s, Portuguese seafarers brought corn to Africa. However, it did not become an important crop in the Lobedu area until the late 1800s. While sorghum and millet are still valued for making beer for ceremonial use, corn has become the staple grain in the region.

Before legislation reduced and limited their land, the Lobedu practiced subsistence farming. This means that the family grew just enough food to eat and kept some livestock. Cornmeal porridge, served as stiff cakes and eaten with a vegetable relish, was the main food.

Ideally, each family had a number of fields in widely separated areas. They planted a variety of

This Lobedu woman is collecting leaves from a pumpkin plant growing among corn plants. Pumpkin leaves are used to make a tasty sauce.

crops to reduce the risk of crop failure should the rainfall be uneven. Drought-resistant sorghum was highly valued when the corn crop failed.

In recent times, the shortage of farmland has increased. Now few Lobedu families can produce enough grain for their basic needs. As a result, they depend on purchased cornmeal.

Good rainfall is essential to successful harvests. Rain is unreliable, however, and drought can cause famine. The great need for rain helps to explain how, in the past, the Lobedu came to rely upon spiritual assistance to bring rain and to enhance the fertility of the land. They held religious ceremonies at harvesttime to give thanks for the first fruits of the growing season.

31

Cattle were part of the traditional Lobedu economy. They remain important to rural Lobedu. Seen above is a cattle auction in the Northern Province of South Africa.

Cattle were important mainly as a form of wealth; neither milk nor beef was a major part of the Lobedu diet in earlier times. Goats provided most of the meat that was eaten. In times of famine, however, cattle were slaughtered in order to trade their meat for grain.

Beer brewed from grain was of great significance in Lobedu society. It was both a source of nourishment and a means of honoring social or religious obligations. Offerings of beer to the ancestors were made more often than sacrifices of meat. Chicken meat was eaten, but live chickens were prohibited in the capital because they were considered dirty.

In the past, when the focus of the Lobedu community was farming, the cycle of work

People dress formally for social gatherings in the capital, such as the one seen here.

changed with the seasons. *Khelemo* (September to January) was the time of hoeing and weeding; *letavula* (February to May) was summer, a time when crops were harvested and food was plentiful; *maria* (June to August) was winter, when the fields were bare.

After the threshing season there was a quiet period in the agricultural year known as *madulahae*, meaning the time of sitting at home, when social activities were enjoyed. Traditionally these were the months for renewing contact with distant friends and relatives. Beer parties and social gatherings were more frequent. Groups of

33

In the dry season Lobedu women decorate both the walls of their courtyards and the floors with beautiful designs. This woman's red paint is made from earth mixed with water.

dancers might be invited to play their reed pipes to the accompaniment of drums. Women enjoyed being at home and had time to renew the designs on their courtyard floors, to grind tobacco into snuff, or simply to meet with friends. This was also the time for making new utensils and building and repairing homesteads.

▼ DIVISION OF LABOR ▼

The division of labor in Lobedu society was roughly equal. Men and women worked together in the fields to grow corn, millet, and sorghum. In addition, women had their own fields of peanuts, beans, gourds, and other vegetables. Wild foods, such as berries and fruits, as well as birds, locusts, rodents, and edible termites added variety to the diet. Men generally looked after the cattle, but women were not restricted from doing so.

One of the most difficult tasks a woman had to perform was using a mortar and pestle to stamp corn into fine meal. This task usually started well before dawn and continued for about four hours. After this she would cook the daily meal of porridge and vegetables. Each wife prepared food for her own household. Women were also responsible for brewing beer.

In general, men worked with metal, wood, hides, and horn, whereas women worked with clay, gourds, and grasses. Craft activities took place mainly in the dry winter months after the cycle of hoeing, planting, weeding, and reaping was complete.

The heavy work of building and thatching structures was done by men. But both men and women collected the required building materials. Women plastered the walls and floors with a mixture of clay and cattle dung. The dung hardened the clay, and acidic chemicals in the dung actually killed germs.

Work parties of men and women cooperated on large projects, often in return for beer.

▼ TRADITIONAL TECHNOLOGY ▼

Today many Lobedu have modern lifestyles. Growing numbers of young people study at college and work in cities. Aspects of modern technology have reached even remote Lobedu villages.

In earlier times, however, most people lived in rural villages and used local materials to meet their practical needs. Iron came from the nearby territory of the Venda people, but most other raw materials were all found in the Lobedu region.

An abundance of useful trees, including the marula and wild fig, provided soft wood for carving utensils. Hardwoods, however, were chosen for building houses. Much attention was paid to selecting the right material for a particular use. Even firewood was carefully selected for its specific heating qualities. For example, firing pottery required a different wood than the kind used for cooking.

From a young age, children learned to appreciate the resources of their environment. They created their own toys, such as spinning tops made from dried fruit peels, and learned craft skills by following the example of their elders. By the time they were adults they had acquired a practical knowledge of useful grasses, woods, barks, clays, and soils. Today many children still make their own toys, but now they mostly use

These Lobedu boys are using wire to make a toy car.

discarded tin cans and wire instead of natural materials.

Traditionally houses consisted of a circle of timber poles, which were held together with cross-supports. This wooden framework was plastered inside and out with mud and then covered with a cone-shaped roof made of thatch. This method was gradually replaced by building with sun-dried mud bricks.

Today kiln-fired bricks and cement blocks are used. Rectangular houses have also become more popular. The old thatching method of layering grass on tightly packed rafters has been replaced by a new technique. Now bundles of thatch are sewn with a long, wooden needle onto a framework of widely spaced rafters.

This homestead below the capital is set on a stepped platform built of mud.

Traditionally the kitchen or cooking house had a reed door, and the sleeping house had a wooden one. There were no windows in these buildings, but smoke escaped through the thatch. Today factory-produced windows and doors are in general use.

When harvests were large enough to produce a surplus, a grain pit, or *kheledese*, was used for the long-term storage of the extra corn kernels. It was lined with clay, covered with a stone or slab, and sealed with dung. Corn on the cob for more immediate use was kept in a *kheashô*, a storehouse made of poles. Unthreshed millet and sorghum were kept in the fields in cone-shaped bins. After it was threshed the grain was stored in large baskets.

Drums have great social importance for the Lobedu. They belong to chiefs and headmen. The drums seen here were photographed at Modjadji's capital.

Metalworking was a specialized skill. It provided tools for farming, fighting, and carving. Iron hoes were used both for farming and as currency. Hoes made from locally smelted metal were soon replaced by mass-produced imports from Europe. Handmade hoes could not compete with imported hoes, but they were still highly valued as ceremonial objects.

Makers of drums were also specialized craftsmen. Drums were not owned by individuals. Instead they belonged to chiefs or headmen. They were used at ceremonies and dances.

Certain drums were regarded as sacred. They were associated with the spirit world, and they

39

were stored in a secret place. They were looked after by a district headman who was appointed by the queen. The well-being of the Lobedu people was said to be linked to the spiritual strength of these drums.

Most women made domestic pottery and the clay vessels used for cooking. Specialist potters produced a variety of fine vessels that were used for grinding snuff and cooking, brewing, serving, and drinking beer.

Family members usually made wooden utensils, woven sleeping mats, grass brooms, calabash vessels, and baskets both for winnowing (shelling grain by tossing it repeatedly) and for carrying produce from the fields.

Factory-made goods have replaced some of these traditional items, but the Lobedu still use locally made products, especially for ceremonial purposes.▲

Specialist potters make a variety of fine Lobedu earthenware. This woman,
Modabodi Molokwane, is polishing a pot.

5

LOBEDU SOCIETY

▼ MARRIAGE ▼

The Lobedu sealed a marriage contract by the transfer of cattle from the groom's family to the bride's family. This cattle transfer, called *munywalô*, was later used to enable one of the bride's brothers to marry. The *munywalô* therefore formed a deep and lasting tie between a sister and brother. In honor of her role, the sister became the spiritual and ceremonial leader in her "cattle-linked" brother's household. If custom was followed correctly, one of his daughters eventually married her son and became her daughter-in-law. A marriage in which a son married his mother's brother's daughter was considered ideal.

If a cattle-linked sister did not have a son, she still had a right to a daughter of her brother's house. In this case the sister might "marry" the girl herself. She sealed the contract for this special marriage using the *munywalô* cattle received when one of her own daughters married. She then appointed a man to father children with the girl. These children took the family name of the sister, which enabled the sister to create a family that carried on her name.

A wealthy woman who had no son to carry on her family name could also create a family or "house" by marrying a younger woman and appointing a man to father children in the name of that house. These examples show that Lobedu marriages are important social contracts, in which cattle play a key role.

▼ ROYAL WIVES ▼

The relationship between Modjadji and her headmen was like the bond between a sister and her cattle-linked brother. Headmen from throughout Modjadji's area sent tribute (gifts) to Modjadji to show respect and to ask for rain. The most notable tribute was to give Modjadji a daughter to become her "wife" (*motanoni*). In this way, Modjadji received many wives.

These women lived in a special part of the capital. They were expected to remain chaste and to serve Modjadji. Those who did not remain chaste were sent back to their families for a time, after which Modjadji gave them as wives to royal kinsmen, headmen, or political clients. A large network of marriage alliances

was formed in this way. This network of relationships played an important role in uniting Lobedu society and in controlling politics.

When Modjadji gave one of her wives to a man for him to marry, he paid no bride-price. Rather it was expected that sometime in the future he would give one of his daughters to Modjadji in return. This kept the cycle of wife-giving and wife-receiving going.

Although Modjadji's reputation was built on her spiritual power to control the rain, her true power depended on her ability to arrange strategic marriages.

Traditionally Modjadji herself lived in relative seclusion. She never married a husband. The father of her children was selected by the royal councillors, and his identity was kept secret. This helped preserve the rain queen's mystique.

▼ STAGES OF LIFE ▼

Different stages of development from childhood to adolescence to adulthood were accompanied by certain patterns of behavior and dress. Special ceremonies and costumes often marked the transition from one phase of life to another.

Traditionally babies and young children wore very little clothing at all—at most some beads for spiritual protection. Until a baby could walk, he or she was carried on the mother's back in a special sling. Before cloth was available, clothing was usually made from goatskin. In this case, the sling was made from the skin of a goat that had been slaughtered to celebrate the baby's birth.

From about the age of four until adolescence, girls wore a small front apron and a short back skirt. Adult women continued to wear a front apron but after marriage, replaced the short back skirt with a longer one. Young boys and adult men wore loincloths made of skin. Hide cloaks were worn for warmth, and sandals were used on long journeys.

From the early 1800s on, cotton cloth was traded in the area. Certain cloths, such as plain black cotton and striped *salempore* from the Indian Ocean trade routes, were made into wraps by Lobedu women. These gradually replaced women's clothing made from animal skins.

From the 1880s on, Christian influence led the converted to adopt Western dress. During the same period, the men who moved to the cities to work began to wear Western clothing. Traditional clothing for men became obsolete by the early 1900s.

In the 1930s few Lobedu women wore any form of headdress. Most women shaved their heads completely. Some wore hairstyles more prominent than those seen today. Unmarried girls often shaved the back and sides of their

This young woman wears a traditional, crown-shaped Lobedu hairstyle for unmarried women.

heads to create a circular crown hairstyle. Today brightly colored cloths, wrapped around the head in attractive shapes, are very popular.

Lobedu women wore hundreds of arm rings and leg rings made from rolled wire. These are still worn today but in smaller numbers. Bead ornaments were worn mainly on special occasions, such as weddings or dances. A necklace made from many strands of old glass beads was worn by a bride and by both boys and girls during the last stage of their initiation into adulthood. A bride also wore a pair of wide armbands made of beads strung between strips of hide. Waist ornaments with multicolored beadwork flaps and girdles made of ostrich eggshell beads were worn for dances. Beads made of copper or brass were highly valued.

Shells from the Indian Ocean were also used for personal decoration. Part of the cone-shaped shell was worn as an ear ornament, and cowrie shells were thought to bring good fortune to the wearer.

All of these traditional ornaments are very rarely seen in use today. The oldest Lobedu beads are still regarded as sacred heirlooms that have powerful links to the ancestors. Among the rarest beads are small, clear blue beads, known as beads of the water. These are occasionally worn individually as protective charms.

▼ INITIATION ▼

Initiation ceremonies among the Lobedu marked the transition from adolescence to adulthood. Though not strictly followed today, in earlier times young men and women went through different kinds of initiation. In addition, some men were initiated into the secret ways of beating drums for rain.

Adolescent initiates were separated from the rest of society for a time. During this period

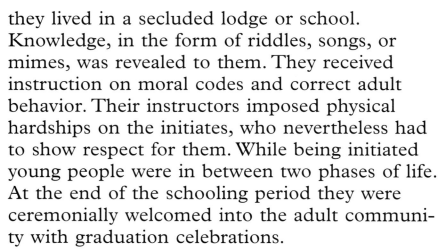

they lived in a secluded lodge or school. Knowledge, in the form of riddles, songs, or mimes, was revealed to them. They received instruction on moral codes and correct adult behavior. Their instructors imposed physical hardships on the initiates, who nevertheless had to show respect for them. While being initiated young people were in between two phases of life. At the end of the schooling period they were ceremonially welcomed into the adult community with graduation celebrations.

Upon reaching puberty, a Lobedu girl underwent the *khôba* initiation ceremony, which lasted about six days. The girl was put in seclusion. She was subjected to harsh treatment from older, initiated girls who were in charge of her instruction and discipline. After this first ceremony, a girl attended at least four or five similar ceremonies for other girls. She was assigned different tasks at each event. Thereafter she was considered fully initiated and enjoyed a privileged status. Real social maturity, however, came only with marriage and childbirth.

Boys' initiation, or *vudiga*, was more formal. The queen, in consultation with district chiefs, appointed the time for the initiation; it was a national event. Boys from different districts gathered together to attend an initiation school that was supervised by initiated men. For the duration of this school, boys lived in a secluded lodge. They participated in a series of activities that ended with circumcision. For some time afterwards, they had to follow certain strict rules, or taboos, and remained apart from the community. They were taught the accepted social values for an adult man. When the schooling concluded the lodge was burned, symbolizing the end of boyhood.

In addition to the *khôba* and *vudiga*, the Lobedu had the *vyali* initiation for girls, the *vuhwêra* for boys, and the *gômana* for men. All of these initiation schools had very strong associations with fertility and rainmaking. These schools were important ways of passing on the values of Lobedu society from one generation to the next.

In the *vyali* school, girls played drums and sang special songs every morning and evening. Secrets about Lobedu society, or *digôma*, were revealed through masked figures and mysterious objects.

The *vuhwêra* school for boys ran at the same time as the *vyali*. Boys learned about the ruling spirit of the *vyali* school. This spirit was represented by a masked figure called *khiudôgani*. Initiates also learned how to make the elaborate *vuhwêra* costumes worn for dancing in the courtyard of the *vyali* school. The costumes were heavy and uncomfortable to wear, but this was part of the hardship that initiates had to

Initiates in the *vuhwêra* school made elaborate costumes, such as the one worn here by an initiate, or *mohwêra*.

endure to became full-fledged members of the community.

At the *gômana* school, initiates were trained to beat special drums. The resulting sounds were believed to please the ancestors and to bring rain. Initiates were taught the laws of the school and received cuts on their faces as a sign that they had been through the *gômana*.▲

chapter

6

THE ROLES OF WOMEN

LOBEDU WOMEN PLAY A KEY ROLE IN THEIR
society. The Lobedu leader is a woman, and
women in general hold many important posi-
tions, especially religious ones.

According to traditional law, women could
own property and hold high office, but they
were not involved publicly in the formal court
organization. In family and other disputes
settled out of court, women played important
roles. However, men ran the formal court
system in Lobedu society. Modjadji was regarded as the final judge in difficult cases, but she
was never actually present in court. Her
absence, however, did not detract from her
authority.

▼ CATTLE-LINKED SISTERS ▼

The importance of sisters lies in the key role their *munywalô* played in their brothers' marriages. Nearly all of the cattle kept by the Lobedu were tied up in marriage contracts. This meant that a man could only acquire cattle by using his sister's marriage cattle. Generally, every brother was linked to a sister whose *munywalô* he could use to marry his own wife and establish a house.

The cattle-linked sister held certain rights and duties in the house that she had helped to establish. She also had a right to claim a daughter of that house for her son to marry. This daughter-in-law (and niece) would bear the heir and help her aunt with domestic tasks, especially in her old age.

After the cattle-linked sister died, the eldest daughter of the family would succeed her as spiritual head of the family. In this role, the eldest daughter would continue to influence family affairs even after she married and moved away.

The eldest son of a man's senior wife succeeded his father as the head of the extended family. He was in charge of handling both the money for the family and their relations with the outside world.

If there was no appropriate male heir, the man's sister could succeed to public office; for

Women play important roles in Lobedu society. These women are dancing for the rain queen.

example, she could become head of a district. This stems from the great emphasis placed on the brother-sister bond in Lobedu society.

▼ WIVES ▼

A married woman was expected to work for her husband's family and bear them children.

At first a young wife was under the authority of her husband's mother. She cooked at the hearth of her mother-in-law, used her mother-in-law's utensils, and farmed the fields of her husband. Later she was given her own fields and grain storehouses, and she had her own *mosha*, or house, made up of a courtyard, utensils, a

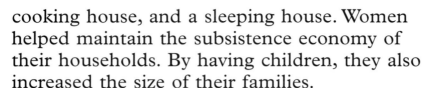

cooking house, and a sleeping house. Women helped maintain the subsistence economy of their households. By having children, they also increased the size of their families.

In a polygynous family, men could have more than one wife. Each wife and her children formed an independent economic unit within the homestead. The husband could not use the food belonging to one wife for the benefit of another. Nonetheless, all members of a large household, including men, women, and children, worked together in the fields at busy periods in the farming year.

Lobedu women played very different roles at home and in public. At home, Lobedu women were responsible for child care, cooking, and managing and growing food for the household. In Lobedu society, this farmwork was recognized and valued. Moreover, women were actively involved in public and ceremonial life.

Although political administration was in the hands of the royal councillors, Modjadji had ultimate control through her links with the ancestral spirits. Modjadji was, and still is, a religious leader whose rainmaking powers are the basis of her political role. Rain is essential to the farming economy and society's security. But rainfall is also symbolic of spiritual well-being and a sign that the society is running smoothly.

▼ THE IMPORTANCE OF RAIN ▼

For the Lobedu, rain is the primary force on which life depends. Rain is symbolic of all that is good and harmonious in nature. By association, damp, shady places and the materials found there are also believed to possess positive forces. River pebbles are buried at the entrance of a village to "cool" the forces of evil that might threaten those who live there. River grasses are woven into necklaces and worn by girl initiates to enhance their fertility. The girls sing songs about fertility and rain. People who have died of certain illnesses are buried in cool places to counteract negative forces.

Coolness is a positive concept associated with rain, health, and prosperity. Heat, on the other hand, is a negative concept associated with disharmony, drought, infertility, and the displeasure of the ancestors. Ancestral spirits that have been angered, possibly by the neglect of their descendants, must be cooled with suitable offerings, lest they send wind to drive away the rain clouds.

Modjadji draws the power to make rain from her royal ancestors. Offerings made at the graves of chiefs or other sacred places are an essential part of rainmaking ceremonies.

Modjadji tells the details of her religious knowledge only to her successor. If rain does not fall, it is said that the ancestors are "holding the

The symbolic importance of women in Lobedu society hinges on ideas of rain and fertility. Even such male institutions as *vuhwêra* initiation are closely connected to ideas about rain. These interesting *vuhwêra* costumes were photographed in 1938.

queen's arm," because there is social conflict of some kind. Harmony must be restored before Modjadji can live up to her great praise name: Transformer of the Clouds.▲

chapter

7

CHANGING TRADITIONS

TRADITIONS BOTH CONTINUE AND CHANGE according to changing circumstances. Past practices are sometimes abandoned, however, when changes are too rapid and too many.

From the late 1800s on, the traditional Lobedu way of life began to change considerably. When increasing numbers of whites began to settle on Lobedu land, the Lobedu people were blocked from their traditional farmlands. The Modjadji Location was established in 1892, which forced the people to move to a small area of land.

At the same time, the colonial government imposed taxes that had to be paid in cash. This situation forced Lobedu men to become migrant laborers. They had to work for wages on white-owned mines or farms to earn enough cash to pay their taxes.

Formerly, cattle had been the main form of wealth, and people supported themselves and their families by farming. When men left their villages for long periods to work in towns, the women took over much of the work previously done by men. They also maintained traditional customs as they had done in the past. In the 1930s the Lobedu were still largely self-supporting.

As the population grew, however, there was not enough land for farming, and people could not produce enough food to meet their needs. Despite access to new technology, by the 1960s subsistence farming was no longer possible; people could not grow enough food to feed their families. Most rural families had to depend on the wages that male family members earned working as migrant laborers.

As a result, the traditional roles of Lobedu wives changed. Families depended on cash to buy cornmeal instead of growing their own grain crops. Some women adapted to the situation by using their traditional skills to earn money at home. They either brewed beer for sale or sold pottery and other crafts. Many other women commuted from their villages to work as low-paid daily laborers on nearby farms owned by whites. The result was increasing poverty in the rural areas. More younger women began to find jobs outside their home villages. This exposure led to new ideas, values, and hopes, especially among the Lobedu youth.

The change in *munywalô* payments from cattle to cash affected the traditional pattern of cross-cousin marriage and the special role of a cattle-linked sister. Today cross-cousin marriage is still said to be preferred, and the *munywalô*, even when paid in cash instead of cattle, remains a contract between related families. The importance of a sister is reduced, however, when her brother can earn enough to marry and no longer depends on using his sister's cattle. Over time this change in the brother-sister bond will probably affect the traditional pattern of marriage. This might reduce the special status of women as sisters.

Although traditional Lobedu values are now under stress, women remain important in the area of religion. Although many families no longer have land to farm, rain and fertility are still important. Rain continues to be an important symbol in Lobedu culture. It represents the goodwill of the ancestors.

In fact, in times of strain and transition, many Lobedu people have held fast to their traditional beliefs. Modjadji remains an important religious leader even in changing social and economic circumstances. However, the future role of traditional chiefs in South African politics is not

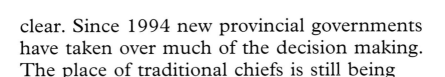

clear. Since 1994 new provincial governments have taken over much of the decision making. The place of traditional chiefs is still being discussed.

The political changes in South Africa and the introduction of democratic rule seem to have renewed the awareness of cultural traditions. Traditions are being drawn on in many different ways to express identity and pride in African culture. Styles of clothing and decoration reflect this trend.

In contrast, during the apartheid era cultural differences were abused for the purposes of seg- regation. The government looked down on the traditions of South Africa's black peoples. Now that all South Africans have equal rights, the many unique cultures of South Africa are being celebrated. Archbishop Desmond Tutu, a South African winner of the Nobel Peace Prize, expressed this new spirit of appreciating cultural diversity. He called South Africa the Rainbow Nation, meaning it is a nation whose richness lies in the differences that it unites into one.

African cultural heritage is now being redis- covered and reclaimed. In looking forward to the challenges of the next century, the people of the rain queen can draw strength from the rich traditions of their past.▲

Glossary

Author's Note: The spelling of the terms follows the old Lobedu dialect rather than the more recent North Sotho spelling.

cycad Rare and ancient species of tree.
gômana Initiation school for men.
kheashô Storehouse for corn on the cob.
kheledese Pit used for long-term grain storage.
khôrô Court of a chief or headman.
marula A kind of fruit tree.
mosata Capital of a chief.
mosha Domestic courtyard; also refers to a household.
munywalô Bride-price; cattle or cash given by the groom's family to the bride's to seal a marriage contract.
polygyny The practice of having more than one wife at the same time.
subsistence farming System of farming in which the family produces all of the goods it needs.
taboo Prohibited behavior.
vuhwêra Initiation school for boys.
vyali Initiation school for girls.

For Further Reading

The few sources that exist on the Lobedu are challenging reading.

Davison, P. "The Art of the Lobedu." In *African Art in Southern Africa: From Tradition to Township*, edited by A. Nettleton and D. Hammond-Tooke, 84–102. Johannesburg: A. D. Donker, 1989.

———. "Lobedu Material Culture." *Annals of the South African Museum*, Vol. 94, No. 3: 41–201. Cape Town: South African Museum, 1984.

Krige, E. J. "Lobedu Marriage and Social Change." In *African Marriage in Southern Africa*, edited by E. J. Krige and J. Comaroff. Cape Town: Juta, 1981.

Krige, E. J., and J. D. Krige. "The Lobedu of the Transvaal." In *African Worlds*, edited by D. Forde, 55–82. London: Oxford University Press, 1954.

———. *The Realm of a Rain Queen: A Study of the Pattern of Lovedu Society*. London: Oxford University Press, 1943.

Kuper, A. *Wives for Cattle*. London: Routledge & Kegan Paul, 1982.

Index

ACKNOWLEDGMENTS
The author acknowledges with respect the enduring work of the late Professor Eileen Krige, and the assistance of the late Simeon Modjadji. She would also like to thank the Lobedu people for their hospitality and kindness over many years, particularly Olga Modjadji and Nerwick Molokwane; and June Hosford of the South African Museum for assisting during fieldwork.

ABOUT THE AUTHOR
Patricia Davison is Deputy Director (Public Programs) of the South African Museum in Cape Town. She holds a Ph.D. in archaeology from the University of Cape Town. Since the 1970s she has done extensive fieldwork among the Lobedu people. Recently she took an exhibition of Lobedu photographs from the 1930s to Modjadji's capital. Her other interests include African textiles and contemporary African culture.

PHOTO CREDITS
All photographs by Patricia Davison © South African Museum, Cape Town, except p. 27 by H. Monnig and p. 56 by E. Krige © South African Museum; cover, pp. 12, 32, 50 by Jean Morris © McGregor Museum, Kimberley, South Africa.

CONSULTING EDITOR AND LAYOUT
Gary N. van Wyk, Ph.D.

DESIGN
Kim Sonsky